NO ONE WALKS WATERS

Books by the Same Author:

NO ONE

WALKS WATERS

by

Daniel Berrigan

THE MACMILLAN COMPANY, NEW YORK

COLLIER-MACMILLAN LTD., LONDON

First Printing

Some of these poems originally appeared in *Ave Maria,
Commonweal, Thought, Sponsa Regis, Woodstock Letters,
Continuum, Spirit, The Catholic Worker, The Christian
Century, Today, Motive.* The poems "Henry Moore in
the Garden," "We Are in Love, the Celibates Gravely
Say," and "This Book" (published under the title of "A
Dark Word") were published in *Poetry* magazine.

To John and Elizabeth
and the Fellowship

Holy Week, 1965

(THE VIETNAM RAIDS GO ON)

For us to make a choice
was always a wrong choice—
why not die in the world
one was born into? what was wrong?

They were patient almost as time.
Their words ate like a tooth.

They looked into our eyes
wild by starts, like the times.
They saw
and marveled, and shook. We saw
out of the edge of the eye
hell;
     out of the center eye
a command, and blinked
their asperges away; *be blind.*

CONTENTS

[*ix*]

[x]

NO ONE WALKS WATERS

The Book

A living eye rested on the book,
it began; *in the beginning*—

it had been blank as pharaoh's head
too smooth for sheltering of ravens

empty as twin wastes of sea and air
until the incontinent seeker, the bird

out of nowhere, out of a passion to know
turning and turning in diminishing hope

above the wastes, seized this bobbing spar
a foothold, a buoy. And the book wrote

itself. For love that it was loved, it began;
was hunger first, was an apple

swelling, reddening, falling—
finally to good use? The book does not know

it knows itself only now in man's guts.

The Writing of a Poem

The greatness of art
is a newborn look, a first cry

or the gaze
the dying summon toward the newborn
held high before clouding eyes,
a flagon, the unpoured cup of going.

Too sorrowful? say then
greatness is exclusions,
ignorance of totems, weights, measures,
woodbins, diets,
midnight arrogance of clocks,
the cat's somnolent metaphysic—

see with a spot I damn them.

The greatness of art; it cries *reality!*
like a mordant blinded god.

Keep the Hour

I set this down toward May midnight.
A blind moon in search of intellect
walks the waste sky in vain. But listen—

the wild kildeer, deprived, importunate
cries, cries out: *man, man is my passion.*

Enough, all said—
the mind's life, an ironic victory
in a stark hour.

Wedding

1.

The mind,
obscure, unenfeebled
above earthly wrack;
calamity darkens,
earth cools like a spent hearth,
stiffens like a wintry sea.

I knew a man, on such a day
led his bride to altar.
Rumor, dreary prophets, concocted dooms?
No. The people, grey in wintry light
took heart. Hands of bride and bridegroom
in singular grace
lay upon every hand.

The world was wedding day.
In the dour sky
stars arose like brides, ignited
by bridegroom eyes.

2.

I saw the bride at her bridal hour, weep
as though heart would break.

What vision woke in her?
Cassandra, Hecuba, ruin
of that fair house she built
stone upon stone, in dream?

What sacred lintel fed the fires,
whose blood poured out, what sons
fell as the roof tree fell?

Unfinished

The world is somewhere visibly round,
perfectly lighted, firm, free in space,

but why men die like kings or
sick animals, why tears stand
in living faces, why one forgets

the color of the eyes of the dead—

The Kings Came Bearing Gifts

Were there humans worthy of it,
poetry would descend
a swan upon the flesh;
first gift.

The second,
a perfect world borne off
by a supernal bull,
the poem gotten.

The third I cannot know
until all heaven's bells
nod in accord
and pitch me into time.

Meantime, the world;
damnation, rot, renewal,

the unexpected
flesh of Christ.

Henry Moore in the Garden

The hard wrought face
of time and human life
that yields to no insolvent poking eye
but is shaped, like infants,
by act and season of love—

I came on this stolen wisdom, Henry Moore,
from your deaf mute
stretched on the earth like Zeus or Christ,
corpse, claimant, porter to hell
couchant on the earth's shield.
When I took his head in my hands
it cracked like an egg, man's touchstone.
The bones shuddered and stilled. He had been lodging
patient as Job's diary
ravens, ambergris, wandering Jews, the deluge.
He spat out Buddha's tooth.

Question that mouth? shout at those ears?
They are not fountain spouts.
They are typography. Period.

The egg of the universe
bakes here.

We Are in Love, the Celibates Gravely Say

They hold Christ up for ascension
like twelve earnest athletes at a trampoline, but

if I go, I return He says
skilled in gravity

which decrees His continuing declension
like dew or fiery napalm

or the seeding of streams with trout eggs.
The twelve earnest orantes hold their hands

safe as stone up to the absent One
which He presently strikes, forces and fills—

world, and world's beauty.

The Leper

In the torrid breathless noon
birds fall like living embers,
their pirate's eye
seizing on some scrap of offal—

they rise straight up with a rat's scream.
The sun hangs suspended, a sword,
a sentence.

Nuns come and go, among the passive sick.
But a leper crouches, face to ground, in the red dust.
He waits.
Waits? the word fails. An alert dignity and repose;
shoulders, arms, head, a young man's pride
a lover's or warrior's limbs.

But the hands? music, art, the subtle gesture
that weaves in air an emperor's clothing
around naked majesty? gentle curious love
parting the world's jungle
to see there (hands see) some virginal
untouched perfection waiting?

No; a botch. Arms the color of old teak
end in crude knobs, as though hands
thrust in a vandal's fire, had burnt back to wrists.

Clad in its white clout
the body, beautiful as a tree
stressed by high wind
(so in its form we see
tempering skill and passion, all at one)

bow, warrior, manhood,
I mourn him. The foul dust stains him
like a slave's stigma. His body falls
(I see it, a year, two years)
a rotten bow,
a bone the dogs own. The clout falls away
the staved body rolls on, its beauty mauled
in time's swollen Styx.

And you redressing Christ, you easter man
I have no more consolation
than a wooden hand could scrawl in carrion dust,
a blind eye compose in the primary world.

The Question

If the world's temperate zone,
then too
its cruel weather,
a punishing torrid and arctic.

If freedom, then two wills
conflicting; wild Cain,
smooth-phrased Abel, too good
for foul actual life.

If shelter and shepherd,
then the wild verge of the heart,
extravagance, violence; the lamb
murdered; rot and stench.

If the way,
then no way at all; way lost
last chance, a Potter's waste.

If gentle vine, then sour lees at heart.

If silence, forbearance
under all malice—

O when
when will You have done
imagining men?

Miracles

Were I God almighty, I would ordain,
rain fall lightly where old men trod,
no death in childbirth, neither infant nor mother,
ditches firm fenced against the errant blind,
aircraft come to ground like any feather.

No mischance, malice, knives, set against life,
tears dried. Would resolve all
flaw and blockage of mind
that makes men mad, sets lives awry.

So I pray, under
the sign of the world's murder, the ruined son;
why are you silent?
feverish as lions
hear men in the world,
caged, devoid of hope.

Still, some win redress and healing.
The horned hand of an old woman
turns gospel page;
it flares up gently, the sudden tears of Christ.

To a Dead Poet, His Book

It is a doorway to seasons; it makes
firm ground for walking, air for sight,
a burning landscape. Have only joy there.

A field of flowers—it is their immortal other.
A crucifix—lector; winter—forbearance;
illness—a transfigured impassioned face

vindicates long suffrance.
Open the book. Wisdom
opens mouth, against all

suppression of death. He is life's
breathing exegete. Take him, I would, at word.

Darkness

Love and larceny plead for it; man could not claim
while daylight guarded, the undefended body—
a full moon's heightening of high fevers,
rising waters unstopped
by the hands' iniquitous and gentle guiles—

no more. I had purposed
a poem on darkness as love's country

but darkness fell, tempestuous.
Stylus, hell's ink, ravens, olive gardens,
climacteric of anguish, my argument now.

Tears too, when man
dumb as an ox lies, death and life
contending him. The ghostly

ungovernable vessel slides in dream;
no, no containing that tide inshore,
that dark voyaging.

O I have questions
for the eyeless Bonze that dwells—

why on death's verge, drink the dark,
why on shore, strike cold fire?

Look; across seven seas, morning's miraculous body.

[*15*]

Air Trip to Boston

1.

I may become
sharp tongued, intolerant, a sore old man.
It looks as though, sometimes.
Still, have stolen from Rouault's art
the old king's fragile unkillable flower.

Heal-all, sweeten my mind's stream.

2.

Turning a page
I came on your death, Connolly,
the fierce, sick crawl of time
a dragged limb or cross.
Then, your hollowed brows
of five, ten years before—
no eyes or face, no particulars.

Rain wash, wind wash, wash of time
leave us little; the brow, a bowl
ground perfect on the earth's wheel

for holding of—what? You, empty, know.

3.

The long line of birches—
landing among them at the airstrip edge,
Russian bells or Saint Elmo's fire
or the plumage of swans;

one voice

flooding the five senses
making truth of the world; *start with us!*

A Pittsburgh Beggar Reminds Me of the Dead of Hiroshima

Seeing the beggar's sign
lettered and hung like a sandwich board—
"I am blind, suffer from angina
and claim no pension or support of any kind."
the crowd dug deep, the tin can
sang like a wishing well.

These days, everyone being at war,
not to pay dear is to prod the inner horror
awake; speech starting up by heart,
lights going on and off like a Greek sky
where five stars make a god; a voice
we got them there; or *he stood like a bastard here, but*
we took him piece by piece;
shipped his skull home, polished like a gouty
whole head—

Perhaps the poem is odd man out
wherein my health like a foulness
drags forward, touches His flesh
an emperor's birthmark
under beggardry, leprosy.
I am too unschooled in gospel to know,
befouled and blinded by the hot droppings
that struck my eyes in sleep, from the great bird
the descending fecal horror.
I stood and shook like ague
—Hiroshima, Nagasaki—
the ungentle names of my memory's youth,

the blue remembered hills
tipping like hell's buckets all their
hot afterbirth on me.

Healer, you would need
stout heart to stand where I must;
no bones, nothing to start with
for repair and solace
of the vast meridian horror.
You would peer and poke
like a blind man on a dump
tracing—another stone in a
dismembered wall—a Neanderthal
boy's bones, half discernible
in turned-up garden litter,
the obliterated dead, the slight
rhythms of marble tracery or flesh—which?

I believe in the Father almighty
and in Jesus Christ
his risen flesh, indistinguishable
from the permeating stench
that rises, swamps, and briefly
drifts on prevailing island winds
when a people goes up, a
mockup of city
slapped together for a brief
sequence—*lights, drone, target*—

Flesh of Christ—
indistinguishable, compounded
yeast, seed, flowering
of flesh of man—
your healing starts here
with the tears the dead

[*19*]

were given no time for, the living
numbed, no heart for.

You, Lazarus, who died and stank—
stagger like a zombie
out of the rubble, jaws
like a burnt carp, unfit for
speech or kiss, that had fed
three days down, on carrion death.

Be first. Arise.
Teach the dead their discipline
—shank, hair, ear, articulation—
that have ridden like furies the inner seas
or fallen
a dew on fleece, or settled
like sandman's gifts
on the eyes of sleeping children.

I toss a coin in the wishing flesh
of beggars; coins in the eyes
of murdered children, for buying of
no tears; a coin
in the carp's mouth for Peter's cast.

The dead too; my coin stand you in stead
who went improvident,
no staff or shift, into time's mountain
as though all
were wide door; this momentary hell
a heaven, and passing fair.

Catechumen

Christ's prophetic soul
stands before history
a blind visionary harper
improvising
time's freedom and sweetness. And lo

divine imagination speaks—
I christen thee
servitor, emperor.

Pray; holy waters never
reduce your untamed heart.
No. You baptize us that
gasp in the world's net,
fish out of element; our milk eye,
our dream, to drift sidewise
in deaf waters; blind,
safe as stone.
Fisher, savior, save from that.

Come and See

Snowmen, birds, the eyed leaves of trees
regard us, the limping dog
on all fours in the gutter after food.

Nothing blind. The mole sees
hard clay is his crystal
where men walk and crawl and fall.

Nothing blind; the full roots are sapient
nerved, eyed, clairvoyant;
a witch will stir a brew I dare you

drink and not change fearfully
in wind and limb and eye,
a mountebank, a baited bear in your

sweet skin. Or a snowman
one black baleful clinker
malevolent upon his creator.

Or a tree; a painted arc
that drank sun, concocted dark
as it took whim. But must see

onset of sawyers, frost, rot—
the crude fall of all empery.

God

I saw Blake's architect
a bearded pagan
calipers in hand, over the nest—

all hopes rode outward
from that thatch of lint and straw
where man shivers night through,
where, if at all, heart must grow human;

someday, if so, be born—
imagination try the world for size.

The Act of Love

In that hour
when the blind body in all its being,
by rare touch of hands and more,
arises healed—

body is one, is more than one
laid upon
by the loved other.
Blood and flesh a seer
need whisper no more; *be,*
and be in me.

But epiphany
is brief as lightning flash;
the flesh, stricken, falls like ripe yolk
apart. Heart, blind again, beats
like hands the thorn.
Dark, dark the world.

Hopeless, lost,
all excellence and indwelling?
love solved, resolved?

No; they have cast in air
roses, burning thoughts embodied,
a winter or summer child
budding there, flowering;
bird, rainbow; *myself, you.*

Fountainhead

The open well
collects leaves, waste, vanities;

then, under careful hands
water runs free again
tideless, endlessly yielding itself.

A stone well
blessed by wayfaring gods
will never dry or sour.

Immortal hands hold the world in cleft
where waters are born; lucid, living, a murmurous child.

The Holy Family Contemplates Ancient Rome

A radiant trinity riding
high above Rome as stars, touching with wands
its pollulent streets, until one by one
like golden kine to knee, temples fall down?

A destroying flame
upon old scrolls, their drying honeycomb? For impure hunger, nothing?

Great kings were born to play at god,
to prey, to auspicate, to haunt dumb nature's glass.
Men sang in spontaneous choral ode
infamy, rotten intellects, all.

But time bore Caesar out;
hands numinous and skilled
to speed or stop the world
                              stop here.

The stone triangulated tent has coped him in.
Fires burn red and blue;
concupiscence, power, an imperial hell.

Cluny Museum

The woman's hands weave
shroud or birth clout in air;
a homely foreign face, a woman
not of any city or countryside I have seen;
a servant perhaps, bowed
with night or dawn labors. And now this death—
heart unfed, hearthstone cold, the beloved son
the single and perfect fruit, crushed under heel.

But a tragic woman stands firm for others' sake.
There is press and crowding of life on her,
even the dead give place. She stands so.

The living son stands too, as this
wooden man stuck through
with a single murderous spike, cannot know. Come,
I touch his wood with news, a wildfire; Rise,
the Lord is risen.

In Memoriam
(G.M.)

A young priest, dead suddenly
at forty years
had taught a metaphysic of the world.
His mind was lucid, ingrained. He would say,
it is deductably verified
that God is immutable; and,
universal order converges on one being.

So be it. This priest, alas for poetry, love and hatred,
was neither great nor evil.
The truths he spoke
being inert, fired no mind to a flare;
a remote world order
of rhythm, cause, finality,
invited submission to his God.

He never conveyed a man, Christ, or himself—
His cleric's eye
forbade singulars, oddments, smells,
sickness, pushcarts, the poor.
He dwelt in the fierce Bronx, among a university's
stone faced acres
hemmed in by trucks and tumbrels. No avail.

Yet it could not be borne
by those who love him, that having passed
from unawareness to light
he should be denied
the suffering that marks man
like a circumcision, like unstanched tears; *saved.*

Heaven is everything earth has withheld.
I wish you, priest, for herald angel,
a phthistic old man
beating a tin can with a mutton bone—
behold he comes!

For savior,
all unsavory men
jostling for a wino's dime
a Coxey's army, a Bowery 2 A.M.
For beatific vision
an end to books, book ends, unbending minds,
tasteless fodder, restrictive order.

For eternal joy
veins casting off, in a moment's
burning transfiguration
the waste and sludge of unrealized time.

Christ make most of you!
like a mother, make man of you,
stitch you through
the needle's eye, the grudging gate.
Crawl through
that crotch of being;
new eyes, new heart, the runner's burning start.

Astonishment

Wonder why illness
an odious plague dispersed,
settles again after deep knives made
of the loved face a tragic mask.

Wonder why after one
tentative promise
raised like a green denial of death,
life resumes
its old mortician method after all.

Wonder why men break
in the kiln, on the wheel; men made of the sun,
men sprung from the world's cry; the only men,
literal bread and wine, the crucial ones
poured out, wasted among dogs. Wonder.

And the lees of men, the stale men, there
in the fair vessels of life, a mock feast;
take it or leave—nothing else in the house.

Wonder at omnipresence of grey minds,
the shade that made
O years ago, ash of the rowdy world.

Wonder at incapacity of love; the heart's
stern pagan ethic, set against Christ at the door
(the discomfiting beggar, the undemanding poor).

Wonder, woman and man, son and father
priest and sacrifice—to all right reason

one web of the world, one delicate
membrane of life. Ruptured
when the ego, viable, red, violent
lunges forward, a murderer by oath.

Wonder.
Transcendent God does nothing.
The Child plays
among stocks and stones
His gospel, a country almanac
records
moon phase, sun phase
hours and elements, grey dawn and red;
He sleeps and stands again,
moony, at loss, a beginner in the world.
History makes much of little; but He
of clay and Caesars, nothing.
There is no god in Him. Give us burly gods
to pummel the world and us, to shake its tree
quail and manna at morning!

Wonder, wonder. A Christ across whose eyes
the cancerous pass unhealed, old evil
takes heart monstrously. What use
the tarrying savior, the gentle breath of time
that in beggars is contentious and unruly,
that in dumb minds comes and chimes and goes
that in veins and caves of earth
sleeps like a tranced corpse, the abandoned body
of violated hope?
Wonder
given such God, how resolve the poem?

Holy Communion

(FOR MICHAEL)

He took his ration
while the lidless spider at ceiling
gathered no moss, alert in stale gloom—
hunger, cold, the ugly staved room.

O if the threads broke, the spider
leapt like a hunchback cretin free
and the net swam down murderous—
would the grail cup then
make miracles for Christ's crew

that is childish in the world, that escapes
day upon day, hell's ambush by a hair?

I stand there steady,
broken bread in hands.
Was it spider thread
or light, light, on dead eyes
crossed my eyes? Lazarus
a moment, did not know, and knew.

Travelers

If geography's the tip of someone's
scholastic needle, we'll ripen and rot there.
But life? even Mona Lisa tries her luck
in treacherous waters. The innocuous stare

warms. Her body cleaves the waters
like time's ripe swan. And the pieta, too long
in stale unanswering air; *whose sorrow
like mine?*—Lady, we've not lived as long

in churches, but we know loss too;
in Queens meadow raise your eyes
from classic grief. The dead
bury the dead, and deep. Come walk our streets. Like Paul

the living sun almost destroyed, that white moth.
He sweated under the cross, the raving
combustible crowd, a hanging or crowning mood.
In dreams, the living eat his flesh, his blood runs
nightlong, a staved cask in those alleys.

My dream beats on. I see the dead
in naked majesty, consumed with longing
for what we in the common street have by heart;
the leaf's errant fall, a child's cry. Delicate,
   brutal, impure, pure—the world, the world
   tears them apart.

Saint Joseph

What draws heart and inner regard
powerfully toward him, is easier
seen than said.

His grace is no breathless mask
under glass kept.

But Saint Joseph's workman hand dying, reaches far
as any man's death, grasps hand there, has gone with us

all, all that sorrowful way.

Man Is an Abyss, Augustine Cried

I saw wild hate and wilder love
murderous, uncontained,
race like a nightmare tumbrel by.

In that fury—
one man of compassion
tossed by chance or providence
among brute beasts;
I am here. What can do hurt
did all the world, at hell's nod, put on
black jaws, cleft hooves, a consonance of beasts?

Adam or Christ, or both;
one face redeems the world.
I saw each stand to the other—
man's folly, man transfigured—
a sinner's sweat
red on the holy face. Father Adam
exulting, topping the savior tree.

And He Fed Them All

Looking out upon that throng
Christ had worked wonders for—

the gentle blind
hearing like fauns
the fall of leaf, the hunters mindless will—

the halt
like marvelous broken statuary;

they come for eucharist, as though rumor ran
in grim autumnal streets
long cold, long unfed

of miraculous loaves and fishes among the dead.

Talisman

I wear
for sign of debt
a silver medal of Christ
sterile of any flower or word,
itself time's flower
molten and hard; the face incised
in the years' acid,
a savior's eye
sleepless, surviving man.

I wear it, a weakling
who kisses the knees of the strong man he fears
and in the dust, may yet
arise to love.

The face turns full profile away—
from time's stinking silver, Judas' kiss?

But a chain swings the rabbi full about.
The face is become
a savior's change of heart.
He turns to me.
I may yet
if silver outlast flesh
die unhanged in bed,
bought, sold for silver.

You too, by the Sea

Life; a vast knot of stinking
wet net, and no nimble fingers to undo it,
no chanty to sing why, no fish
headlong, bullheaded to jump in and be

my congregation, my fish course—
No. But blue Monday by the sea.

The addled buoys dong bad luck by heart,
the sea stinks like a shored shark
malice in his man's jaw—*one more, only one more.*

Tired anger, bone weariness
colorless, graceless, dumb—

Nevertheless, the fisherman casts off

as if on sea
(or heart, or forehead)
an artery forked and ran—

a god's trident raking out
like sea lightning
some uncharted tragic way.

If

If I am not built up
bone upon bone
of the long reach and stride of love—

if not of that
as stars are of their night;
as speech, of birth and death; thought
a subtle paternity, of mind's eye—

if not, nothing.
A ghost costs nothing.
Casts nothing, either; no net,
no fish or failure, no tears like bells

summoning across seas
the long reach and stride of love
dawning, drowning those black waters.

I Encounter Men in the World

hopelessness stands in their eyes,
a dry despair, hands broken upon stones,
an eroded life.

I think then, of a young mother
her child in arms, a concentrated inwardness
as of a sea shell coiled, its music
self-composed, self-given.

I long at sight of sick men, to induce
—as a shell drawn from seas
generative, uncorrupted—
some birth their tears had not dared come upon.

Year of Our Lord

(ALGERIA, 1961)

Turmoil, day labor,
opaque mystery no resolve may lighten—
a slave's or beast's portion
in worst hours. Life sickens,
dull blades make havoc of true order.

Purest act fails first. Imagination, trust,
spontaneity, heart's saving warmth, where?

I walk out, appalled
by day or night.
Somewhere a man dies in the camera's eye;
men like carrion dogs sniff, shy, prowl.
I long to stand in that picture, to kneel and drink
at a god's fountainhead.

World spins like a headless top,
butchers put up their shutters,
Caesar in dreams sucks red thumbs clean.

The Sistine Chapel

Illusory, a maelstrom of wrong purpose.
I would whitewash the whole.
Then, in favor of religion,
place there for a poverello's sake
for his gospel eye, Cezanne's *Card Players,* say.

See, the painter cries, *God*
is that meditative peasant
or the watcher brooding over; He is
like us, all said.

Divine things
need only look human. The cards deal and fall
fair as leaves or creation; we are in good hands.

Sorrow

I saw a mother mourning her sick child
the hundredth time that day, or any day or night
equally wearying, equally hopeless.
She sees death stand at the end of days.

And saw a young husband serving the Mass;
his wife, suddenly dead, borne to that altar,
he, pouring wine and water,
impassive, cold at wrist and heart
to match her cold, one ice laid on one flesh.

The exemplary world moves us to tears
that in their falling, purify
eye's glance, impure world, both.

I know the world better now, if world has face.
It beats steadily as a child's heart.
It is the moon's rhythm that like a woman's long
unutterable glance of love, draws the bridegroom after.

The Poem

When I see flowers borne into a city room
arranged there by hands
I am urged inward
through the gross slag, the filth and pitch
to the heart of life.

Amplitude, warmth, saving compassionate grace—
the flowers beat and beat on. The divine ship;
its sails
silken and tough in the wind
beat and beat on. The poem
is the journey toward.

Last Day

When He did come, all the
folderol in the books burned like faces
for shame. Imagine the world
not catching fire, that had no other
reason or being, preachers cried like frogs.

Not a sleeper's hair turned, not one.
Where the living dwelt, He took breath; where the dead
lay cold as stones, or stood, long stones on end,
He troubled none alive. They were safe from Him.

It was more like the sun's fiery mind
or a woman's hands, compassion. Not one
dull standing autumn weed denied

its windless hour, warmth and seed. He was not named
storm.

Ironies

Time's white-maned river
bearing all before, a loud
welter of hooves and water
over scoured rocks.
Doubtless here, thick-sown
ironies for the fisher
who hauls up in lucky hour
a wrought augustine carp
jeweled of eye, scored
by cunning hand—
icthys, the sacred fish.

And doubly ironic
the golden sunset bird
at a fork of the grove
a darkening spectrum, giving
lacklustre day the lie,
immortality
in the day's setting eye.

But peacock and fish
dredged from groin and vein
of the world's cardiff body
have small resurrecting power
for the ridden heart.

I remember a man dying;
his hand cold as coin
in mine. I would, in onrush
of sorrow, have given all

all I had won of life—
No. Life stopped short
at thinning breath.
He grew cold in time. I wear
for talisman, him.

Song

(from jacopone da todi)

In my morning prayer
I saw *love* written
upon every creature

men on their foreheads
trees on their leaves
houses on their walls.

Christ has flowered in man's flesh
let human nature rejoice!

Prague: Old Woman in the Street

In the country saying, she was only
doing what must be done, as a stone falls
or a wheel turns. Her body punished
by a man's labors, to man's hard shape.

Childbearing done, not for twilight peace
but for this; pulling a cart, sweeping cobbles
stolid in the killing cold. Suffering?
hands were made for it, blood warmed to it.

I tell you, I stood stupefied
as though a flare went up in the foul street,
some ikon Christ casting rags off for glory.

Woman I never knew, I kneel to you
I am born of you. For you, my heart keeps
like an unhealed leper's, stint of hope—

Christ is not hard as stone, cold as my doubt.
You neared. Unbearably, the quick dead cried out.

Lines

A peace treaty signed
across the dead body
of a great man;
excellence, holiness,
radiant style of life, all
liable to process
of inert minds; trial by epithet,
execution by irony, burial by despisal;
overmastering fear of action, time
gutted of substance and surprise;
suppression
of protest and anger in the human furrow;

and love, great love, who is the heart's
daystar and oracle,
whose teasing marvel is
touch me and be,
who walks the bestiary mind
lion and lamb, man and woman, one—

great love forbidden utterance and act.

This tears me, as wild horses
in a mad dream ran wrecking.
Or worse—in a dream of waking, stood
horrible, at large, real in the world.

For Ivan Mestrovic

(HIS STATUARY; JESUS AND THE WOMAN
AT THE WELL)

Old epitaphs
chipped by ice and fever
falling to no use—

Nevertheless, rejoice to see
imagination
catch in vials
the last breath of the dead

to make of air an eye, of wind an ear,
of space, articulated arm and hand
to pluck the dead by the hair, to stand, to push them
toward.

I saw in Notre Dame park the old man on his stick
pausing upon bronze Christ, thirsting upon His thirst.
No source could slake him; no, though the woman's vessel
were a human heart; its salt sweet,
its water wine, under that bridegroom word.

Moment

Is the world then, more
than an animal haunch, cleft
under the butcher's ax,
a world hung raw, flayed on a hook?

Is the world more? is it
five or six deer together, standing in dusk
abstract, momentary; then startled, dissolved in
newer and newer rhythms, mauve hoofs, red nostrils
eyes unwary as first stars?

Are we, the watchers
bathed in that sight, a baptism?
The world
for all its stern exactions, loved us once:

homeward in dark, pondering *what is the world?*

A Young Bird Found Dying, Brought Indoors

The moral of this
is slight and adventitious; the bird
had never mastered air, and of earth
drew in no health, but a foul humor—
now he lies blackening
any dead childish thing
untried by the world.

Earth mother—
tender, plangent, taking all to breast,
(children, great heroes, beauty, intellect)—

so slight a soul
lies light in a ghost's hand. Grant it
breath, passage to morning;
a furious phoenix brightening of hell.

How Strange the World

Richness, strangeness, depth; I see
autumnal birds in woodgrain;
the heart's skin, thin as sight
vatic as drumskin;
a drummer's ten fingers,
love, hate, brushfire, beaching of that scow
crammed like a pod with seed of
universal hope, animal and man—

the fingers; ten stars, conflagrations, seas—
I ride on them.

Dachau Is Now Open for Visitors

The arabesque scrawled by the dead
in their laborious passage,
leaf and flower mould of their spent bodies,
faces frost touches gently and coldly
to time's geometric—

a multitude of skeletal men
presses forward; such cries
the patient poor speak, whose despair
leaves no man's peace intact, no coin
for death's foreclosing fist.

In the Children's Ward

I was pondering no mystery
and far in mind from mystery's
Necromancer who, time gone,
made five flowers grow
in consecrated ground,
lit five candles in a ghost's hands and feet.

Merciful men and women stood appalled
when the Lord sank and died; a crowned head
must, if it rise intact
make a fiery circle around; all
stand without.

I thought as I bent
to innocent blind faces
how inmost sight refused my face; linen
ripped like graverot; eyes
no tears burned black, met mine.
And pity died—the feeble child
my childish nightmare made
of rickety bed and doll.

All, all wrong.
Sight was blind. But the children
moved dexterous as fireflies, in a blind
garden of broken hands and dull minds.

I Fear Most, I Think

    if nightmare is oracle—
not madman death
not quartan fevers
nor the long litany hell composes
of unstrung jaws, their fiery diatribe

but dreaming or waking—
that child
pale as mushroom, blind as night fog

no grace, no stance, no name—
shuddering, lame, befouling the world.

Compassion

I sing bronze statuary
enduring rain and cold,
eyes alert to cast back
the sun's burning shafts,
cavalry drumming the dead awake,
a fisher's net soaring,
a snare
to catch worlds in.

But in November rain
—rotting asters, scum of leaf—
I came on a dying man.

His eyes pled
like an animal at the block
I am come to this? And I
in the rotting asters, sick at heart
must kneel upon squalid ground
man's defeat striking
marrow and heart;
Unless I suffer this, you
gentlest Abel, strike
with a glance, Cain down.

PARIS SUITE

1. A Beggar, First

Sometimes, misery has beauty to commend it.
I saw a poor man bedding down
in the midnight street, coolly. He might have been
gorgeous Louis preparing levee.

Weather stood austere,
late goers homeward, pinched, intent.
The beggar made his bed as best
rags, leaves, torn paper might. De Gaulle's

disgruntled snowman face
crumpled under head, made a pillow
like ambergris
floating the brain gently nightlong

in a grand savory sauce
of power and rhetoric. Human life
flickers inextinguishably in the jungle street.
The beggar, annealed in dignity

settles back
in rags his dignity weaves new.
He takes up in cold hands
tattered Molière; those cunning civilized hands

that lifted, veil on veil
the quintessential ironies of mind,
that fleeced the rich to very clout, that hailed
great Jove in rags

crown him at midnight.

[*61*]

2. Our Lady of Paris

The mother, frail seeming as flesh
fled or stood fast
as providence decreed—
a beast's croft for her son,
Herod's sensual fury, then
1789, the enthroned whore's flail.

Now, under the vault's held breath—
wax flowers, dank spiritless robes.
Mother of exodus, her cold hands take
of this world no comfort.

Tonight, the stinking Seine
leaps the quay stones, takes living flesh
in morsels. A gypsy
mother and child might dream
four walls and fire; and Mary
white faced at door for shelter.
Always, the poor—

Dives screams in his stews,
his tripod of burning bones.

3. Certain Concessions

You are not the golden Greek sea, no
Shakespeare never slept here—
granted, the nightingale can be heard
only in Versailles tapestry;

starting with stern exclusions
I end as always
helpless in praise;
marvelous architect of man; mind's life that
transubstantiates to poetry.

Cast words away. The city, the
egg of Venus, halves into all things.

4. Unfinished Lines

October scuds; leaves come down
in great sheaves, a scythe blade crossing the eye,
a net upon the Lord's miraculous word

or the first lines of poems that
on other winds return to other groves,
mate new plumage, stand hard in mosaic
icthys, the Lord had luck here.

A bronze head of Mallarmé by Picasso—
the true burden of falling leaves.
Does man live only in thought? Where are his hands?

Who cares? great lines crown the brow
that crowns its quiet grove.

But how clasp hands with the dismembered dead?

No one's familiar. Listen and look long.

5. Saint Sulpice

In the botched barracks, coming on
a marvelous suave Christ; thigh to wrist, one great line
of contending death and life, the wood
golden as time's honeycomb—
                              stuck out of sight for
being guilty of beauty
                    as though in some
grimy back yard, a scarecrow stood
and withstood, and in spring arose
caparisoned as Spring Christ with trumpet vine.

6. A View from a Side Street

The streets shouldering awkwardly along
like flower carts of blooms
all sight and bestowal—

windows like blank eyes
starved
for one burning realizing blue—

Walk out
some night that sacks your sight, like a
condemned man's, in suffocating black.

Be lucky, a star falls, cry out *I see.*

7. The City Undertakes a Restoration of Public Monuments

How much life do you allow us?
We breathe and breed
and blink equably into dawn or dusk.
Beasts do as much. But to be free

passionately, without base despisal.
Unlike stoic marble, covertly grinning
behind masks on All Souls' Day;
to admit death and beginning

taking that blow like any woman
exulting in her child, her brow wet
with birth or death sweat, she scarce
knows. *How much life?* she mocks death.

I would in the wandering city
make in my mind that phrase
new, anew; despite
time's cruelties, that belabor

innocent men, clear expectancies.
I walk and seek. Algerian workmen
with steam hoses, burnish new
the scarred animate bones of Paris.

8. Paris, You Could Press Wine from Thistles

make easter eggs of gutter stones.
Your metaphysical butchers chop and chop,
time's neat headsmen. Irony and grace
hold like a lifted shrug, all life in fee.

What unlikely thing is not your poem?
one leaf in Luxembourg gardens
trodden, dried, a simian brown.
But hold it up; a fan, a lover's lattice
to say through to the world
if you stand there in brown twilight, I love you.

Or follow history back;
in defeated November, dense chestnut alleys
carry the mind's dark and bright
interminably on; a chorus of blind seers
fires men like brands, extinguishes them
with a coping hand.

City whose stones stand—
naked queens the lions guard, saints, poets' heads
on bronze pikes. Garden upon garden of birds
make present paradise, make heaven and hell
a dull stale cage.

9. The News Stand

In cold November
the old man stood
like a stone man, all day
in a flimsy canvas box
of struts and patches; a lung, a world
billowing with big portentous names.
And the stone man stood;
eighty years, voice drumming like a god
wars, death, time's bloodletting and getting.

At sundown the world came apart,
a shack of cloth and board, roped, hefted.

Last, rolled up his pages; the leonine faces
snuffed without a cry, dead as all day.

10. A Thrush in the City

Supple as a fish
or a violinist's hands
the thrush
fans out, ascends,
paying to gravity
the tribute of grace

not as a parasite
I drink of you earth mother
but standing at height
to pour like a gold mask
poetry on your wounds

11. Immanence

I see You in the world—
venturesome children, their cries and gestures,
the sharp sad whistle at six, the emptying park,
flybitten leaves, embers of the magnificent
weathered candelabra, the poplar lanes.

Yet faith asks, like a shaky woman, some epiphany—
a renaissance cock calling Peter's sin
from the Pantheon roof, shocking the crowd's ease,
sinking the children's fleet

that now make alas, as life does, a silly wayward wake
or none at all; and no one walks waters.

12. Air Mail Letter

A brutal landscape
is relieved among the blind
by hand given to hand.

Since that mysterious hand
ikons and saints speak of
seldom if ever deigns
miracles, interventions,

I write in hope
of casting measure of light
on your dark and mine.

Or, to brighten the image
I saw once, a procession
of halt, blind nuns;
on Corpus Christi day
they wove of flowers and leaves
a road of procession.

The dark fell; the nuns'
bodies swung like vanes
and weathered it. Their eyes
triumphant, ravaged, held
life's acid ironies.

I carried the Host that day.
They in the doorway singing
floated in peaceful midstream,
a foil of swanlike forms
gentle, but on a sudden

[72]

steeling upright, turning
intent, unappeased, to me.
Come cried the virgins *despise
vain emulation, the childish
time-ridden heart. Bring to birth
in one flush of being
intelligence and love.*

The moment passed. They were twelve
defeated women, singing
Pange Lingua. Slowly
entered again the dark
portal of horn or ivory.

These occurred to me—
gentle adherence to love,
hope beyond reason of hope.

The procession moves toward you.

The Test

With serious intent, He created
man to His image, to make test of this
body He claimed of Mary.

Let there be man is one thing—but
let there be this, my hangman? Yes,
no turning aside of nails. I
appoint you to my flesh.

The hard fast rule, cried nails in Him, *is love.*
Climb me, taste me, cried the tree.
I am heavy, crown to limb
with harvest Him.

Making Something

The blind man longed passionately to see
but the wish was vain
while dawn delayed
a false savior, conferring no sight
from his miraculous store.

The cripple dreamed
dancers and tumblers all night long; at dawn
he lay there, dumb as the world's wood or winter,
no volcanic man.

Tears were his only poem.
He spread out
like a blind fakir, on the mat of the mind
his sorry magic;
two scored stones for eyes,
broken sticks for limbs,
for man—
sans eyes, sans hands, a century's
empty locust shell. For oracle, only
be content, be like.

Forty-two

Come passionately into life,
inhabit the world
like a beloved body, intact, invaded.

Alas, no; man lives
neither caught up in Danae's cloud
nor taking joy of some fierce sacrifice;
but sodden, unlovely,
half murdered or born, dragged to his hour.

The Jewel
(AT A LECTURE)

The lady wore a jewel
green and wild;
her mind burned and knew
and turned, astonishing, upon us.
We saw the gem was intellect,
the gem as gem
an unmixed motive, literal and paste.

We will recover, lady, your mind's jewel
time eases off bone, a late
blossom from branch. Better; brides toss away
like overlong virginity, their holy flower.
All humanity is bridegroom, wears you for bride.

This Book

As I walk patiently through life
poems follow close—
blind, dumb, agile, my own shadow,
the mind's dark overflow, the spill of vein
we thought red once, but know now, no.

The poem called death
is unwritten yet. Some day will show
the last, first line,
the shadow rise,
a bird of omen

snatch me for its ghost

and a hand somewhere, purposeful as God's
close like two eyes, this book.